W9-CNA-989

Stupendous Sound

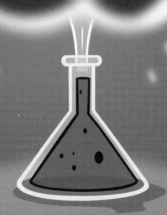

by Nadia Higgins

illustrations by Andrés Martínez Ricci

Content Consultant:
Paul Ohmann, PhD · Associate Professor of Physics · University of St. Thomas

visit us at www.abdopublishing.com

Published by Magic Wagon, a division of the ABDO Publishing Group, 8000 West 78th Street, Edina, Minnesota 55439. Copyright © 2009 by Abdo Consulting Group, Inc. International copyrights reserved in all countries. All rights reserved. No part of this book may be reproduced in any form without written permission from the publisher.

Looking Glass Library™ is a trademark and logo of Magic Wagon.

Printed in the United States.

Text by Nadia Higgins
Illustrations by Andrés Martínez Ricci
Edited by Jill Sherman
Interior layout and design by Nicole Brecke
Cover design by Nicole Brecke

Library of Congress Cataloging-in-Publication Data

Higgins, Nadia.
 Stupendous sound / by Nadia Higgins ; illustrated by Andrés Martínez Ricci.
    p. cm. — (Science rocks!)
 Includes index.
 ISBN 978-1-60270-280-6
 1. Sound—Juvenile literature. I. Martínez Ricci, Andrés. II. Title.
 QC225.5.H55 2009
 534—dc22
                        2008001609

Table of Contents

Sounds Around You

Shhhhh. Do you want to hear a secret?
Then close your eyes and listen.

You might be surprised by all the sounds around you.

How a Sound Starts

What made these sounds? All sounds begin with something moving. The moving thing goes back and forth very quickly. It makes a vibration.

A bee's wings flutter fast.
The wings go *bzzzz*.

BZZZZ

Your Voice

Whisper. Sing. Shout! What makes your voice?

Two folds of tissue stretch inside your throat. These are your vocal cords. When your breath passes over the vocal cords, they vibrate. That lets you talk.

How Sound Travels

Drop a pebble into a puddle. Ripples spread out from the pebble in circles.

You can't see sound. It moves through air in invisible waves. The waves move outward from a vibration like the water rippling outward from the pebble.

In outer space there is no air. That means there's no sound, either.

Unlike ripples in water, though, sound travels in all directions.

Jump into a pool. *Smack!* The sound travels across the water's surface. But it also travels up toward you.

Into Your Ears

Boom-ba-boom boom! Fireworks explode above you.

The sound carries through the sky, down into your ears. It makes a flap inside your ear vibrate. This is your eardrum.

Sound moves fast. It takes a sound about one-third of a second to travel the length of a football field!

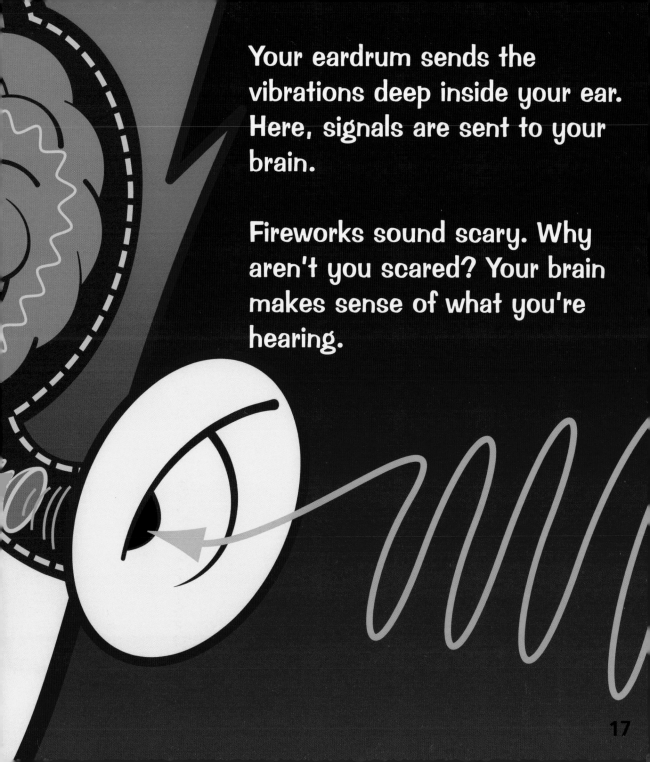

Your eardrum sends the vibrations deep inside your ear. Here, signals are sent to your brain.

Fireworks sound scary. Why aren't you scared? Your brain makes sense of what you're hearing.

17

Loud and Soft

Vroom! An airplane lifts off the ground. The sound is so loud you can feel it in your stomach.

Loud sounds are made by big vibrations.

BROOOMMMMMMM

People who work around loud sounds wear earplugs to protect their ears. Loud sounds can damage your ears over time.

19

Zzz, zzz, zzzz. On a still, hot day, you can hear a fly buzzing against a window.

Soft sounds are made by small vibrations.

High and Low

Pluck a harp string and it vibrates quickly. It makes a high note that sings across the room.

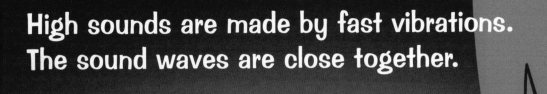

High sounds are made by fast vibrations.
The sound waves are close together.

As people get older, they can't hear high sounds as well as they used to. You can probably hear sounds that are too high for your parents' ears.

A bass guitar's sounds are low. Its strings
vibrate more slowly.

Low sounds are made by slower vibrations.
The sound waves are farther apart.

Echoes

Stand across the schoolyard, facing your school. Shout your name. Did you hear your name again? That was an echo.

There's a pause between a sound and its echo. That's the time it takes for the sound to travel to an object and bounce back.

Echoes happen because sound waves can bounce. The sound of your name bounced off your school and back toward you.

Stupendous Sound!

What's the difference between a noise and a sound?

A noise is a nuisance. But sounds are stupendous! What's the most stupendous sound you know?

Activity

Sound in Action

What you need:

A sheet of plastic wrap

A large, empty container
such as an empty coffee can or a cake tin

A rubber band

A spoonful of sugar

A lid to a pot

A large spoon

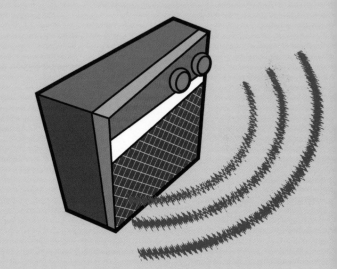

What to do:

1. Stretch the plastic wrap over the top of the container. Secure it tightly around the container with a rubber band. (What you're making looks like a drum.)

2. Sprinkle the sugar on the plastic wrap.

3. Hold the pot lid a few inches from the container. Bang the lid with the spoon as hard as you can.

4. Watch the sugar move! What is making the sugar bounce on top of the plastic wrap? It's the sound's vibrations!

Fun Facts

Some bats cannot see well in the dark. They use sound instead of sight to find prey at night. As a bat flies around, it sends out very high sounds. The sounds bounce off insects, then come back to the bat as echoes. By listening to the echoes, the bat can tell where to find its dinner.

A human heartbeat is one of the lowest sounds we can hear.

We almost always hear sound waves through air. But sound can also travel through liquids, such as water, or solids, such as steel. Sound travels faster through liquids and solids. It travels almost 4 times faster in water than it does through air—and 18 times faster through steel.

Some airplanes can travel faster than the speed of sound!

Lightning makes thunder. When lightning flashes, it heats the air around it. This causes the air to vibrate and make sound. Thunder and lightning happen almost at the same instant. So why do you often see lightning several seconds before you hear thunder? Because light travels much faster than sound. You can tell how close a storm is by how long it takes thunder to follow lightning. If it takes a few seconds, the storm is far away. When the two happen almost at once, the storm is upon you.

Many sounds are so high, people can't hear them. Some animals, such as dogs, bats, and dolphins, can hear sounds that are too high for human ears.

Glossary

eardrum—a flap of tissue inside the ear that vibrates when sound waves hit it.

echo—sound that has reflected, or bounced back, off something.

nuisance—something that is annoying or unpleasant.

vibration—a fast motion back and forth; the origin of a sound.

vocal cords—folds of tissue inside the voice box (or larynx) of the throat that vibrate to create a person's voice.

On the Web

To learn more about sound, visit ABDO Publishing Company on the World Wide Web at **www.abdopublishing.com**. Web sites about sound are featured on our Book Links page. These links are routinely monitored and updated to provide the most current information available.

Index